For the Love of Words

For the Love of Words

*A Book of Poetry
and
Short Stories*

VENISIA GONZALEZ

Copyright © 2013 by Venisia Gonzalez.
Illustrated by Shawn M. Malone

Library of Congress Control Number: 2013902574
ISBN: Hardcover   978-1-4797-9353-2
                Softcover   978-1-4797-9352-5
                Ebook   978-1-4797-9354-9

All rights reserved. No part of this book may be reproduced or transmitted in any form or by any means, electronic or mechanical, including photocopying, recording, or by any information storage and retrieval system, without permission in writing from the copyright owner.

This book was printed in the United States of America.

To order additional copies of this book, contact:
Xlibris Corporation
1-888-795-4274
www.Xlibris.com
Orders@Xlibris.com
115974

Contents

Inner Peace 11

POETRY

DARK

A Break from Madness 17
An Uninvited Guest 18
Bound 19
Clean Air 20
Demons 21
Do You See Now? 22
Here Before You 23
His Anger, His Disease 24
Hollow 25
How Much 26
Journey 27
My Abyss 28
My Life as a Wandering Soldier 30
Need for Sorrow 31
No Home 32
Now You Listen 33
The Decision 34
The Killing Fields 35
The Room 36
What 37
What Am I? 38
Without Light 39
Words 40

GRIEF

It's Time	43
Missing	44
My Celebration	45
Peaceful Silence	46
Take Me	48
Time to Be Me	50
Why Is That?	51

HEARTACHE

Alone	55
Angry Now	56
Blind	57
Cry For You	58
Entombed	59
Hurts Me So	60
No Good	61
The Tango	62
There Was Once . . .	63
Turn On the Light	64
Who's To Blame?	66
You Used To . . .	67

LIFE

Death, the Journey	71
Do I Have Your Attention?	73
Evaluate	75
Fighting Now	76
Let Go	78
Light	79
Mother	80
Silent Clown	81
Stand Alone	83
The Doll	84
The New Me	85
The Routine	86

Unchanged 87
Waiting 88
What's Wrong? 89

LOVE

Destiny 93
Fearless Passion 94
Finally Found 95
For You 96
Forever and Ever 97
Found 98
Just Know 99
Love Is a Struggle 100
Needing 102
New 103
Passion 104
Passion and Love Within 105
Proof 106
Remaining Strangers 107
See You 108
Their Fire 109
Thoughts in My Head 110
Well, Should I? 111
What I Remember 112
What Must I Do? 113
You, Me, Bliss 114
Your Waters 116
Yours 117

UPLIFTING

A Doggie's Heaven, a Doggie's Love 121
A Great Day 123
Candles 124
Celebration 125
Change of Plans 126
Dr. Seuss, My Seuss 127
Enchanted Awakening 128

Heaven's Arms 130
I Still Do 132
Is This 133
Linger 134
My Pocket 135
Nature's Beauty 136
Oh, Space, My Love 137
Peace 138
Petals 139
Rebirth...140
School Days 141
Sisters Are..143
Sullen Journey...144
Take Some Time..145
The Night's Welcome 146
Welcome Back...147
You Are My Drug..148

DEDICATIONS

Her Image 153
I Miss You 154
If I Should Fall 155
Imagination...156
Isabel's Calling...157
Looking at the World through His Eyes 158
My Munchky 159
Six Candles 160
Tearful Silence...161
The Team 162
Without Saying...163

SHORT STORY

Abuse 167
His Calm..170
She's Hurting...172
Truest Love..173

To my wonderful sons,
for whom I am honored to be their mother,
Kaelan, Dimitri, and Anthony,
and also,
in memory of my daughter,
Isabel Simone.

To my daddy, Ismael,
who never stopped believing in me.

Shawn,
thank you for pushing me toward
my dream.

Inner Peace

You rise, you fall,
You sleep and you wake,
Take in the sorrow and joy with every breath you take,
Remember that with every step
You're alive, and you're someone who can
make a difference
For remember, it's not how long you live,
it's how you choose to live that counts.

Poetry

Dark

A Break from Madness

You can feel your heart beating through your chest
Feel your temperature rising
Adrenaline pumping through your veins
Your head ready to explode
You stand on the edge of a cliff
You scream with all that is in you
Spreading your arms above you
Screaming louder until the only sound
is the echo that it makes
Release me
Take the blade that's been thrust inside your being
Unleash me
Tear away the chains that bind me
Lay your hand upon me
Withdraw the pain and rage that lies within
I have seen hell and torture that encases your every being
I have walked through the abyss of fire and terror
Give me freedom, for I have fulfilled your request
Grant me solace, serenity
Clear the voices that run amok in my mind
With a wave of your hand, it can end
It must end
My task for you, completed
Grant my release that was promised to me
Lift the darkness to let in the light
Set me free
Madness to a gentle calm
Peaceful mind
I have done what you asked of me
Grant this warrior discharge with honor
To begin anew
Finally in peaceful rest.

An Uninvited Guest

"Hell hath no fury like a woman scorned"
Some say it's true
What do you say?
Man's God is righteous and merciful
He has a plan for everything, so they say
This God doesn't ask if his plans are good with me
A mother's most precious treasure is taken
"To return to heaven"
My pain, my torment, my agony
Anger raging inside me
Cursing his "Almighty" name
Do I have a seat by your side?
I give what's left of my soul for her return
Will you grant my request?
What price must I pay?
I will pay with my blood that drips from my wrists
My wound is deep
I ask for no savior, no forgiveness
I bleed deeply
My smile only for you
My skin burns, and yet I feel no pain
Warmth drips upon my body as I bathe in this red sea . . .

Do you consider me a follower
or
Just an unwelcomed guest?

Bound

Mirrors and mirrors
Reflecting no image of myself
No longer visible for lack of a soul
The cold darkness echoes upon my skin
Breath visible in the chill
Cannot bear this embrace of icicle pain
This blackness is the darkness of my tomb
In meeting death, I lack the faith to open my eyes
The song, once sung, now closes
Words no longer vibrant in the strings
Choked by sadness on this moonless night
Black hair tangled as if tangled thoughts run through my mind
Body bound by sorrow
Abandoning my body.

Clean Air

Do I tear myself apart?
Why do I blame myself?
The world can be cruel
I must still survive
No confidence in my decisions
So many mistakes have I made
They cannot be undone
Oh, my heart still yearns for him
Why do I love the one who hurts me most?
I'm not alone
Why do I feel that way?
Torment inflicted on myself
I can choose to let go
I cannot untie the strings
I've been caught in this web for so long
I cannot break free
Slowly I succumb to this feeling
Must break loose
Like chains too broken
To struggle to the surface of the water
I must breathe the clean air again.

Demons

Shadows of images
Stars in the heavens
Flesh upon flesh
Pleasure in sinning
Evil eyes do I have
Wicked is the smile
It is within.

Rage is the emptiness
Hate is the weapon
Feelings are few
Power the controller.

The laughter is hollow
Hand is the messenger
Imagine an answer
Inside lie demons.

Do You See Now?

Pain and torment have spun their web
No longer allowing their life to pass
through the silken thread of what once was
My loneliness shields out the warmth
that once embraced my every being
The cold and dark anger
Hatred has laid its cloth upon me now
Not able to free myself from these chains that bind me
Chains that I have
made with every poisonous tongue
I've allowed to pass through these lips
Words like daggers that I have
so deeply embedded into your skin
I am no longer the face that you remember
I am the creation of what has grown from your darkness.

Here Before You

Alone I had sat imprisoned within a room
The dark and cold sealing my tomb
Roots had sprout up, trying to trip me
My true feelings were lost somewhere in history
For they were lost in my lifetime of misery
Too long they were hidden
Feeding on my pain
My heart was handcuffed with a lie
For you were king and I your queen
I am strong
For I have lived
A lifetime of memories no longer in chains
Those tears will not have spilled in vain
Through every step that I have fallen
I stand again with fierce eyes
Without tears left to cry
The sweat on my brow
No longer from pain and fear
Determination is what I feed upon now
Underneath the stars and moon
I swear, for I am no longer the fool
I rise upon the glimpse of dawn
Taking in the sunlight's warmth
No longer does the dark shadow stand behind me
Before you, I stand renewed
I am now the warrior.

His Anger, His Disease

Like a fire without warning
He explodes into flames
His temper uncontrolled
Can no longer be tamed
Ignited by fear, jealousy, desire
His raging flames can go even higher
His words, like a serpent's tongue
Both savage and cruel
Escape from his mouth
Rendering you unable to move
Tears fall from your eyes
Yet you feel them burn
His two-sided disease
Put out the flame or let it burn?

Hollow

In my darkness
There is no sound
Silence echoes through these halls.

In my silence
There is no light
Suffering echoes through these halls.

In my pain
There is no salvation
Screaming echoes through these halls.

No motion left
Tears dried up
Blank canvas to rest the eyes upon
No color, no sunlight, empty.

Venisia Gonzalez

How Much

How many things can one do?
How much can you carry on your shoulders?
People say that you don't get more than you can handle
Do you believe that?
I can say I don't agree
So much do I carry
So much do I deal with
Does it make me stronger?
Who knows?
I've been weakened with my woes
Dropping to my knees
With tears spilling upon my cheeks
As if heavy rain within a storm
I ask why
I can't handle all that I face
My mask is all that one sees
I hide my pain with a smile
Act as if everything is fine
I keep moving forward
A car driving on fumes
I cannot afford to fill the tank
I need help
None comes my way
What do I do?
What do I say?
I struggle to face my children each day
No answers, no help comes to me when I pray.

Journey

Screams of pain from the masses
      that lay upon my feet
The heat and stench of the rotting flesh
Predators begin their feast
I look upon the ocean
Battle on the seas
Scent of salt and blood in the air
"Push on" is the voice I hear
Helmet, hot and heavy
My arms aching
Sweat pouring down my back
      with the blood of my enemies
"Push on"
"Push on"
No time to rest.

My Abyss

Emptiness is growing
The light is dimming
Air so thick, it chokes me
Feelings so deep inside
Locked away.

My vision is blurry
Getting worse as time goes by
When I close them, I see the light
Smell the salt coming from the sea
I hear everything.

Roaring, crashing
The sea or inside me
On the edge of an abyss
The unknown below
See nothing.

I open my arms
Feel the wind brush upon me
I want to fly
See the world from above
I am free.

Guide me
Hold me as I soar
Feelings hidden
Emotions, my adrenaline
I leap.

Release my voice, my spirit
Allow my emotion to break free
I no longer want to be locked in my chains
The chains I've made myself
I've lost the key.

Is it clear to me?
Am I hearing what needs to be said?
Do I step forward?
Do I release what's locked deep within?
I may have found the key.

Venisia Gonzalez

My Life as a Wandering Soldier

I'm a lonely soldier
On a distant land
Crying to my father
With blood on my hands
Can you hear me, Father?
I sit on your right hand
Calling out for you
I'm in pain.

Need for Sorrow

I am a magnet for sorrow
I long for the drama
Need it like a drug
My constant fix
It began when she died
When I became ill
Or from the ashes of an abusive childhood
Surround me with attention
I find the tears
I find the ill choices
May I have my fix now?
Do you see me ache for the sorrow?
Give it to me
Let me bathe in its sour waters
I cannot go a day without it.

Venisia Gonzalez

No Home

Home is where the heart is
Or so they say
My heart knows no home
Knows no warmth
No fulfillment
No joy
Hardened by the cold of the world
The icy winds that blow like hurricanes
Treacherous waters that consume my soul
I'm a glass statue left on the rocks
Awaiting that last push, so I shatter
Shatter into pieces to disappear
        as if I never existed.

Now You Listen

I'm writing out to all those who think they know me
Guess what, you don't
For years and years of pain
Molestation and the rape
The abuse and all the lies
You claim you never heard me cry
Begging not to go back there
You turned away from me
Going on like I'm a ghost
I don't exist
To you, I'm just a person who you can toss
I've been through hell and back
Five times it took to bring my son back to life
My daughter, now she's dead
This cancer eating me away
No phone call, no cards
You only call for your stupid game
Trying to drive me insane
Don't want to hear your empty cries
Your selfishness, your twisted lies
Call for information on the others
Are you kidding?
My life has been turned upside down
I've suffered in ways no one should
I can't believe you told my kids
Your empty promises and heartless grins
"We'll be there," you say
What a joke
Stay away from them
Stay away from me
Pretend we're dead, we don't exist
You've done good playing that game all along.

Venisia Gonzalez

The Decision

Inspired by a line by Nissmech:
"What follows life is most certainly death."

What follows life is most certainly death
It is a journey we all take
At a point in time
The mind ravels in thoughts of what is to come.

Does it matter what life you lived?
Can the choices paint a different picture?
Will you transcend to another being?
The mind can cause confusion of your thoughts.

Sadness and grief can change a destination
If allowed
It will control you
Every part of your being.

The soul must travel
Beyond different worlds that cross each dimension
Will you see it come?
Are you blind to its light?

Darkness may roam unto the path
Will you justify the words from within?
Can your voice speak with such a cunning tongue?
It has come to this crossroad.

What follows life is most certainly death
Will you be able to make that cross?
The cross into the world you must choose
Light or darkness—the soul must speak.

The Killing Fields

The Killing Fields are left to slumber
Soaked and rich in garnet's water
Darkened angels slither among the festering corpses
Deafening silence thickens its mist
Tortured souls walk along the earth
Dark, violent visions inhabit what was once human
Electric surges fading as the heart stops pumping
Swaddled now within Death's blanket
Unheard screams through nightmare-filled eyes
Hell's doors closing with tormented cries.

Venisia Gonzalez

The Room

My eyes open into darkness
The cold, dark room—
        I am surrounded
My mouth opens
No sound emerges
No doors
No windows
The cold hard floor that lies beneath my feet
Fear
Fear that begins growing
How did I come to awaken here?
My mind, it races
Thoughts of escape—but how?
I am surrounded by nothing
Fear has placed its veil upon my head
The pain so great
It brings to my knees
My head
Inside, the pain so constant
Never to surrender its hold
Help me,
        someone must help me
Yet there is no one to listen.

What

A whisper, a secret, a shadow has turned
Has turned on those who ask it to
A darkness, an emptiness beginning to grow
It grows as it's told to
A night, a black night with an uneasy rest
Fallen upon those who need not ask
Pain, a sharp pain inside my ears
The venomous words now drain from me
Take this uneasy circumstance
Banish it down in depths of loneliness
To hear no cry, no ache, no moan
To never venture in that time you've left behind.

Venisia Gonzalez

What Am I?

The light peeks in
Walls are my prison
The windows tease what I cannot have
They sing songs to remind me
I'm trapped
The light squeezes through
I reach with my hand to feel its warmth
Speckles in the light feel like messages of freedom
Never looking for a door
Looking outside
I see the people walk through the day
It slows in the evening light
Nothing to break the glass
I scream so that someone will hear me
I only hear silence
No one can see through the glass
The dark shadows aren't images of me
I'm a ghost that hasn't moved on
I need to find the stairs to lead me away.

Without Light

A hole
A hole in darkness
An endless pit
No light
No breeze
No rope to escape
Moans and screams
My voice, it echoes
The blood, it runs from my fingertips
My nails broken from trying to climb
My skin peeling and raw to the bone
Aching, burning as if acid was poured upon my hands
Clothes tattered and torn with no way to fix
Deeper and deeper my body sinks
Struggling to grip the nothing surrounding me
The dark, so dark
The dark and cold
No sun, no moon
No light.

Words

No one believes a word I say
The information I give is false
My parents have never told the truth ever
So the finger gets pointed at me, anyway
Words running in the air
None are told to me until after
Everyone just blaming me
The truth doesn't even count
I don't have it in me
I'm tired of fighting
I just can't anymore
Who'll believe me?
Only God knows that my lips speak the truth
That's not good enough
Is it?

Grief

It's Time

Kiss, kiss
My heart so full of love,
        my heart feels like it will burst
All I need,
        I found in you
Spilling out of my affection for you
How I've always wanted it to be
To have my baby here with me
Your gentle fingers
Your tiny toes
Your beautiful face
I smile and I glow
I said I love you
Just held you close
I sang to you as you slept
Cherishing every last second
Thank you for letting me love you
Thank you for choosing me
I'll always be with you
As I know you will be with me
Again, I said I love you
It was time to say good-bye
That was when I bit my lip
As tears streamed down my face
Gently and slowly your heartbeat fell silent
Together we'll forever be
My heart beats with the memory of you.

Missing

Mystic magic lies upon the sea
No more pleasures are known to me
For you have traveled beyond my reach
You have no words,
      can no longer speak
Your memory vibrant in my mind
I imagine your smile a thousand times
I treasure your things
I miss your scent
I cannot wait till we meet again.

My Celebration

The holidays are empty
Hollow in their sounds
No smile for me
No laughter in my heart
Just a hole
A missing part gone
Try to try
No strength to move
Pain causing me unable to move
No longer the smile
No longer any meaning
Just the emptiness
Missing her consumes me
My heart and soul
Tears inside
Screaming in silence
Longing for her touch
A smile, a laugh
The smell of her hair
Silent wishes to be unheard
Not to be granted
Accepting this change
Difficult to swallow
Unable to move forward
Presents not to be given
Sight of her joy and surprise
No longer in my vision
Holidays no longer the same
No longer fulfilling
They're just more painful
Harder to celebrate
Harder to enjoy
No taste for their anticipation
Just gone.

Venisia Gonzalez

Peaceful Silence

I look in the mirror
I see myself
Tears and sadness
This pain revealed
In this reflection
I see your shadow
Your hands on my shoulder
Slight glimpse of your smile
Warmth overwhelms the ice in my blood
I take a deep breath
Tears fall
My heart aching
Your grip tightens
I feel that I'm not alone
I fall into your arms
Your embrace allows me to cry
Cry harder than I ever have before
Your gentle hands lift my head

I look into your eyes
I catch my breath
I ask you, "Why?"
"Why does it hurt so badly?"
"Why do I feel broken?"
"Why am I lost in this night?"
"When will the sun rise in your soul?"
Your gentle fingers touch my face to wipe away my tears
You do not speak
You only smile
Your gentle kiss upon my forehead
Again our eyes meet
A soft warm breeze do I feel
I close my eyes
I take a deep breath
I open my eyes
Gently the darkness reveals the sun
I smile
You whisper, "Be at peace, my love."

Venisia Gonzalez

Take Me

Reaching for your hand that is no longer there
Longing for the smell of your breath
Visit me in my dreams
Smile and laugh for me
Why did you go?
I am so lost without you
My soul crying out
Tears overflow at the view of your face
Remembering you everywhere I go
Why were you taken from me?
Heal my heart, for I cannot do it alone
Reach for me
An angel's hand to eternal beauty
My gateway to the heavenly light
I pray for you to find me
Kiss my lips and let me know you are with me
Embrace me with your tiny arms
Laugh for me
Your voice is heaven to my ears
Why can't I be with you?
Will you come for me when I leave this world?
Will we be together for eternity?
Will we play amongst the clouds, the stars, the moon, and the sun?
Will I wake to see your face?

Fill my heart for it is broken
Lay beside me as I sleep
Take me to where you are
You are my path to the light
I love you, my creation of pure beauty
I love all that you were
I cannot heal
No sleep
Constant sorrow
Never will I forget, for my pain is permanent
Guide me
Save me
Reach for my hand
Grip tightly
I can never let go
Time won't change anything
I love you
I love what you gave me
I despise your absence
Come back
or take me with you.

Venisia Gonzalez

Time to Be Me

When I dream of you and me
Waves of emotion wash over me
Releasing anxiety and worrisome care
In my arms your heart stopped beating
The machines went silent, no more beeps was I hearing
They came into your room and said you were gone
It felt like the craziest thing I had ever heard
Uncontrollable emotions not comprehending
My mind only filtering those words as I dropped to my knees
Then they reached in my arms to take you away from me
Desperately trying to hold you, to keep you with me
They repeatedly told me to let go, for you were dead
Trying so hard to clear those words from my head
Overwhelmed by all parental fears
I'd sell my soul for a couple of dimes
To change what happened, to reverse time
My heart now fractured, for that decision could never be mine
My heartache turned into hours, months, and years
Trying to soothe my soul and mind
Five years I have mourned you
After the struggles and hardships, I'm finally mending
Praying that love and peace wash over me
The sound of your name travels on the gentle breeze
Your love pours out onto me, open and free
Sometimes I can feel you next to me
Saying a prayer to heal my spirit that needs to be nursed
I thankfully know that you are in peace
It is now urgently time to be . . . just me.

Why Is That?

Is hope learned?
Instilled at a young age
Or just a fantasy
Fictitious story to feel better
It can be torture
Cause the anger and pain that follow its failure
Can a prayer be heard?
How do you know it'll be answered?
Does it get chosen like a lottery?
Pick the magic numbers with a purchase
How deserving you are
When you beg with all your heart not to take what you treasure most
To be able to switch places
Why give a beautiful treasure only to take it away so shortly?
Why would some Almighty figure be so cruel?
Is it his game?
To tease your heart
Like dangling candy in front of a child only to take it away
Is it fun to be mean?
Not fair when the love is so deep
So treasured, worshiped, adored
How could you tear my heart from my chest?
Do you get satisfaction?
Put a smile on your face
I hope you're happy
You broke me with your cruelty
Take my joy away and my health
My boys only to suffer more
Enjoy yourself
I cannot look at you
Magnifying glass over an ant in the sun
That's what you did
Why is it that you can still have a following?
Do you deserve it?

Heartache

Alone

Letting go is a knife in your stomach
So painful but has to be removed
How'd it get to that point?
Where'd it go wrong?
In my heart and in my mind
I search for answers I cannot find
Tears fall endlessly from my eyes
He no longer feels the same
I don't know why
I did everything right
Put up with his ups and downs
His wrongs and rights
Tears and smiles
Yet here I stand in a pool of tears
Empty promises in my hands
Alone in pain and in love.

Angry Now

Your words like knives
Stab in my gut
Didn't think about what you said
You didn't give a . . .
For so many tears
I cried over you
My heart was left broken
Broken over you
You walked away
With a smile on your face
You heartless . . .
Pointless of tears
Not worthy of my love
Not worthy of my time
Spoke of forever
Serpent's tongue's lies
My heart weakened
Softened by your unspoken vows
I'm no longer the fool
I'm angry now.

Blind

Memories of days gone by
Feeling the breeze kissing skin
I reminisce of what once was
Dreaming of love so true
A love that was once me and you
In my heart, a treasure you would find
This unconditional love unlike any other
This love, my love, was meant for you and no other
I had run to you with open arms
Allowing the passion within me to unroll
You screamed aloud, "Don't come one step closer"
"The lies I have told you have no end"
"I have only longed for your physical touch"
Hearing those words
That's when I should have said good-bye
I couldn't
I wouldn't
All of me belonged to you
Tears of my ruptured heart echoed
As if chimes making music in the wind.

Venisia Gonzalez

Cry For You

You are far away
I am still here
Memories are all I have
In a shadow, I see your face
On my knees I pray
Looking in the mirror
Tears upon my face
Holding your jersey close to me
I scream
I beg you, please
Please come home to me
This distance between us
Holds me in chains of depression, of misery
You
You are everything in my heart
My soul and body are yours to control
Do what you like
Please do
Tears and memories
You have spoiled me
That smile
Oh, I cannot forget
Your wisdom and grace
Oh, that beautiful face
Looking in the mirror
Staring at lovers in the park
On my knees I pray
I
Cry for you.

Entombed

Lips that drip
Sweet honey words
Trap me into your
Spider's web
My straitjacket tightens
In this cruel love's asylum
Forever I'm entombed.

Hurts Me So

Aches and aches
It stings
Bleeds without end
Shattered
       and torn
Too good
Too good did I do
Yet punished
Torn down were you
"I need to put me first," said you
Badly bruised were you
"Not myself," said I
Such pain and loss have I
She was taken . . .
       Still asking why
Change your tunes, do you
Say one and another, you do
"Always take the blame" did you say
My heart belongs to you come what may
Change your words yet again
Found another, yet we still are friends
"Different roads did we go"
"Different one I now choose"
My road always followed yours
My heart forever remains with you.

No Good

Can I feel?
I've hardened what I showed before
So many words have punctured me within
Despair, torture, no love
How long must I endure?
Years and years of neglect
Am I not worthy?
Always tossed aside
Wanted only at your need
I should close off but always open to you
Why can't I stop?
Not answer when you call
I know you will never see me
See me for me
Love me for who I am
What I've become
So proud
The words I long to hear
Just one time
Begging to be accepted
Your first
Nonexistent in your eyes
So many tears have I shed
Wishing you'd change but deep within I know you won't
Why don't you love me?
How many times will you hurt me?
Why are others more important?
I am your daughter
I don't exist in your eyes
Your calls are just for what I know
Contaminating everyone around you
You won't change, will you?
No hope for our relationship to grow
I'll never be good enough
Never in your eyes.

The Tango

All the same
Your words
Your actions
Nothing has changed
You express your love for me
Yet all you cause is pain
I'm hurting
Can't you see?
Too weak to play these games
I stand on the edge of a battle
The battle within me
No time to play your game
I have much work to do
No longer can I dance with you
This tango of torment and deranged love
We stroll across the pieces of my heart upon the floor
You lead
As always you lead
I cannot be your partner any longer
My soul in need of fresh air
I walk off the floor
I walk out of the room
Don't reach for me
No longer am I yours
No more of this tainted tango will I dance with you
No more.

There Was Once . . .

What did I do wrong?
To make you want to walk away
Five years with you
Five years I gave
To be with you every single day
On my mind day and night
Sleeping in your arms I remained
The love we made always extraordinary
A kiss from you made me fly
A kiss from me for you felt the same
All things in common
Best friends, lovers, devoted friendship
I did everything for you
Push and encourage you
To see in yourself what I saw in you
So again I ask
What did I do wrong?
Did I love you too much?
Once you loved me the same
Not once did I not love you
Even at the worst I believed in you
No matter what others said
My love, strong
Now still strong
Yet not for me from him
There was once . . .
A man who loved me more than life
Who wanted me to be his wife
There was once.

Turn On the Light

My lips are dry
Barely any moisture in my mouth
Foul taste on my tongue
I thirst

My lungs gasping
The ache of being crushed
It suffocates me
I cannot breathe

My eyes swollen
The sting upon them
It hurts
The tears keep overflowing

My heart aches
The pain within my chest has consumed me
Its agony
The feeling that it's been torn from me

I scream without a sound
I shake
I tremble
I fall to my knees
I call out your name
You cannot hear me
I reach out for your hand
You cannot feel me
I cry tears in your name
You cannot see me

For the Love of Words

I love you
I need you
I long to hear those words again
Whispered sweetly
I crave for your gentle kiss
Your touch
The smell of your skin

Your loving arms that held me
I desire our passionate embrace
Hear you call out my name
I call out yours as we tremble from love's ecstasy

Come to me, my love
Our promise of forever
Knowing you were the one
I shall not betray
For my heart will always be true
You are what I desire

My thirst
My reason for breath
My tears
My aching heart
All stem from you, for you
My soul incomplete without you by my side
As if stumbling within the dark

Please turn on the light.

Who's To Blame?

All the love I feel
Equal to the pain I feel
How do I react to that dilemma?
Do I let go?
Must I hold on?
My heart weakens with every harsh word
The words "I love you" no longer have their meaning
I long for you
I call to you
The pain, my expense
I weep tears stained by false hope
The illusion of our perfection
Believing your empty promises, your empty words
I don't know how to let go
I know I should
I know I need to
But still I cannot
Why do I allow this torment?
My heart so conflicted
Do I enjoy this dance of what we've become?
Is there a part of me that believes deep inside I deserve no better?
Must I turn the blame onto myself?
I could've made it stop
Turned you away so many times
But I didn't
I've allowed it to continue
So I am at fault
      but you share the blame.

You Used To...

You used to enjoy your time with us
Video games and movies
Hanging out and laughing
Smiling we were all happy
You used to.

You used to take your time being with us
Not watching the clock and rushing
Taking your time and hugging
Smiling we were all happy
You used to.

You used to enjoy your time being with me
Holding me tight and snuggling
Kissing my forehead gently
Brushing your hand along my body
You used to.

You used to love me and hold me dear
When I fell, you'd wipe my tears
Kept me strong and silenced my fears
Making love to me and nibbling my ears
You used to.

You used to make me promises you never did keep
Wanted me silent, to not make a peep
You hurt me and broke me, now I can scream
Told you a miracle grows within me
Told me, don't make a scene
I told you I love you, still you turned your back on me
I believed that you'd love me
I believed that you cared
Alone I face this journey, our miracle I choose to keep
Before now, you'd be happy
You used to.

Life

Death, the Journey

Some people say death is permanent
The final page or chapter
It's like going to the hospital
The sterile smell
Smell of death and decay
A doctor going to a designated room
to tell a family of grave news
Yells and tears
Screaming and sorrow
Those left for the aftermath
Death leads to your body in a box
Six feet under you lay
Body begins to decay
Some people say that when you die,
    the soul is free
Free of its shell
They say that right after you die,
    the soul visits their loved ones
to let them know they're okay
Others believe that when you die,
    you just die
No great kingdom with gates
Yet the argument is and alleged testimonies claim,
    that there is a great light
Could it be the light in the hospital?
A light in the ambulance or in a car?
Is it better to know that you're going to die?
Or is it better not to know, to be sudden?
When it's sudden,
    there's too many things left unsaid

Sometimes no reason explained for the death
Too many questions
Nothing prepared
If you know,
        does it cause more pain?
False hope?
The agonizing struggle
The pain
The cost
How many treatments or doctors will it take?
Your family watches you in agony
Slow and painful
Maybe no pain
Just time
Time to put things in order
Time to say with all your heart, the things you long and need to say
Time to say good-bye
Death is just the ending
Or is it a new beginning?

Do I Have Your Attention?

Can they not hear when I say no?
If I want to be bothered, I'll come and visit
It's not like THEY come over
Don't they get that I want to be left alone?
Their comments
Their judgments
Haven't they done enough already?
I don't need you to hold my hand unless I ask
Not a child to accompany to the doctor
You don't need me to attend to you
Tired of being "told" on what they're going to do with MY health
It is MY health
My journey
I don't need to be pacified
I don't need to hear the words again
Will hearing it from the MD make it sound better?
Would watching me in pain be satisfying? Or how about vomiting?
Would that ease your concern?
Did you consider me for once having to watch you boo-hoo?
Would respecting my wishes be too much to ask?
Too many hands in the pot
Spoiled, burned, rancid smell of disarray
Can they not hear when I say I need to do this alone?
Can I keep my privacy and dignity?
It's about me, not you
When did this become a committee?
They make comments like hypocrites
As they keep their lives in the closet
Why should I be the fat lady on display at the circus?
To "ooh" and "ahh" or hear "boo-hoo"
I'm done with that
Call me bitter
Call me stubborn

That won't change a thing
I'm grown, not a baby
Let me be with my dignity
Accept what I say and do
The decisions are up to me, not you
Be mad all you want
Won't change my mind
I'm cemented in place
The wind can howl for as long as it likes
I cannot break
I'm immune to your words
Respect or stay away
It's me in the driver's seat
      and I have the keys.

Evaluate

Question your existence in the universe, to which would heighten the validity of every decision, every word, every move you've made.
Makes you think . . .
Do you rethink of all that has occurred in your life and question if this path was predetermined?
Is "love" a valid feeling or a word that, by many, is thrown around too freely?
When your heart aches, is it real or an illusion of pain?
Tell me.
Make me understand why.
Why do I long for the sound of a voice?
The "one"
His voice
Was this chosen for me?

Venisia Gonzalez

Fighting Now

Lyrics to "If Today Was Your Last Day" by Nickelback
Muse for my poem

> *My best friend gave me the best advice*
> *He said each day's a gift and not a given right*
> *Leave no stone unturned*
> *Leave your fears behind*
> *And try to take the path less traveled by*
> *That first step you take is the longest stride*
> *If today was your last day*
> *And tomorrow was too late*
> *Could you say good-bye to yesterday?*
> *Would you live each moment like your last?*
> *Leave old pictures in the past*
> *Donate every dime you had*
> *If today was your last day?* (Nickelback)

I knew it from the very start
My fear and loathing have had their fill
From life I thought I'd never part early
Destroyed by the doctors' poisonous dart
For what purpose, what reason, why?
I was completely shattered and torn apart
I felt as if I was trapped within a net
Was this really a huge mistake?

Felt trapped in a straitjacket, tied and restrained
My head in my hands, confused, crying
My emotions put to the test
I'm trying to hold on so desperately
The rain hiding my tears that fall again
Protecting those around me with a lie
No longer can my feelings and the truth be contained
Feeling my life was so beautiful, now feeling like a dream
Can someone help me pick up the pieces of my shattered heart?
My love of life was once so divine
Divine light blinds me, I cannot see
I hope I still can see the sun and rise with inner strength
I'm now fighting for my life.

Let Go

Diseases are invisible
      Leeches that cling to us
Anger becomes their voice
It's when you realize that death
      is only the beginning
To a beautiful new journey
      that not everyone can follow
Where there is no more pain
No suffering,
      no despair
No hatred,
      jealousy,
           racism,
                or
                        malice in content
Then and only then
Can you let go and be free.

Light

Vacant and cold
I was wounded
Wounded with questioning what's false and true
Wordless suffering
Wondering what's fiction and truth
Alone feeling restless with death's kiss
Imprisoned by longing to have one last look
Your vision so bright, lighted the way from my darkened tomb
I couldn't think of anything more beautiful even if I tried
The memory of an ocean so blue
I'd have sailed the sea to reach you
Gazing from the shore
Grasping at clouded hues of nature's view
The gates of heaven
Nearer to me now
Your face in this dream has guided me
Your whispered hand has led me
Your blossoming voice has soothed me
Spending this tranquil moment with you
As I rise to greet the morning sun
I am draped with light and peace.

Venisia Gonzalez

Mother

What do you do when your child is in pain?
His tears
His eyes all strange
The terror he shows as he looks at you
The violent shake
His body constricted
Fluids expel from his mouth
How do you feel when you hear all the sirens?
Needing to show no fear in your eyes
What do you do?
You stay strong
Focused
Keeping your head straight
Calming his fears
Reassuring he'll be okay
"Mommy is with you"
Don't be afraid"
Everyone is nice, there to help him
There to make him get better
Hospital admittance
"A special hotel adventure,"
I tell him with a smile and a laugh
Silly faces do I make
Silly jokes I tell him
Underneath this mask I'm scared,
yet my face smiles
What do you do when your child is in pain?
Be his mother.

Silent Clown

You can't make people understand
Exactly how you feel or what you're going through
They want to believe anything else but the truth
They tell you that you're negative
In reality they're the ones in denial
The pain every day, every week, every month
It grows more each time
Vision affected
Ability to walk more difficult
Sleeping through the night no longer possible
Pills and treatments
They're no better
All they do is break down what's left inside you
Weakening your ability to fight
My humility extended by the thinning of my hair
Crying in silence
No one can see my agony
Fevers consistent
Burning inside, the outside freezing
On top of it all, the nausea
Can no longer bear the smell of food
To allow its taste to touch these lips
They have no idea what it's like
Faking my smile, my jokes, my laughter
Can they not see?
I'm as transparent as a veil
My shoulders struggling to bear my load

Venisia Gonzalez

What to do next, my children, their future, my grief
So much to handle alone
No faith left in hoping
Again they say negative
I say realistic
Secretly hoping to one day see my son's future
Praying they don't find me in an eternal sleep
Yet no longer do I want them to witness my agony
My oldest trying to bear some of the weight
Determined not to lose the grip of my hand
I smile for I have raised him well
So much love I can't leave behind
Oh, my pain so great, so vast
Tearing my body in pieces
Tears in my eyes
I hide in the dark
Placing my clown before me.

Stand Alone

Beyond the seas
I see my reflection
Wondering where it'll take me.

Do I stand alone or take the leap?
To ask for your hand to join me.

Will I be afraid of what I can't see?
A coward not having any faith in me?

I shall stand strong
I'll stand on my own
To venture on the journey before me.

Venisia Gonzalez

The Doll

See it still
Silent
Beautiful
Its porcelain skin, flawless
Eyes, a brilliant blue
Hair, perfect—as if coming from a salon
Clothing, well selected
She stands in her case
Protected from harm
Alone and isolated
Her perfection is her curse
Her silence, her enemy
For so long as stone
Never with a voice
Never to feel the warmth of people
Must break the case
Allow the air to pass through her lungs
Screaming for all to hear
"I am not fragile"
"I will not break"
"I have strength"
Feet, solid like stone on the ground
A fierce heart
Finally defending itself.

The New Me

Tired, so tired
Every day the same
Energy is disappearing
My hair is so short now, I look like a boy
Medication causing weight gain
I thought it wasn't supposed to
The nausea is still consistent
I'm so afraid and closed off
I feel alone every second
Everyone tired of my ordeal
I can't believe they are my family and friends
I am truly alone with my children
My dog, Dobie, listens to my cries
Licks away the tears
Snuggles to give me comfort
I depend on him so much
My additional reason to smile
I couldn't make it without him
Do I sound like the "cat lady?"
The loser with no friends
The pathetic female who needs help for everything including remembering
This is the "cancer" me
And I am alone and strong.

Venisia Gonzalez

The Routine

Every day, the same routine
Alarm clock, kids, and pills
Getting dressed, breakfast, bus stop
Waiting for the bus to come
Driving to the doctor
One of many
Co-pay's a never-ending bleeding wound
Tests and scans
Urine and blood
IVs, injections
Lectures over and over again
Come home exhausted
Nauseous and dizzy
Pain just aching with no relief
Smile a fake smile as the children enter
Trying to hide my grief
Struggling through homework, dinner, and conversation
Reading a bedtime story
Showers, teeth needing brushing
Inside crying for relief
Asleep are the children
Ending of my day
Crying in silence you'll find me
Praying and praying
My illness, a cure
Tomorrow is the next same day.

Unchanged

I patiently sit in the room
Awaiting the results of my test
The scent from the doctor's office is always sterile, cold, permanent
I sit in the chair twiddling my fingers
My leg sways back and forth
Hoping for a positive comment
From a white coat, pressed and clean
I don't know how I arrived here at this destination
Everything is pretty routine
Pain, nausea, sleepiness
To go through a day feeling like myself
Feeling "normal" would be a triumph
Every day is the same
Not much different from the next
To become enraged at how it's come to this
Would only be a waste
Waste of time and precious energy
Writing is my escape
My institute where all feelings are kept
My emotions are on file
At the door I can enter and leave if I choose
Here I am in control
Is my frame of mind correct?
Maybe yes
Maybe no
Frustration and pain that continues
God, allow me to grasp at salvation
If for just a little while.

Venisia Gonzalez

Waiting

Sitting and wandering what's going on
They say a few hours, but is something wrong?
You hope for the best
Faith is your test
Laughter and remembrance to keep you at rest
Reading and writing to occupy your time
Getting food in the cafeteria, patiently standing in line
Soon it'll be over and it'll all be fine
Waiting patiently, words of hope telling you it's now over
Simply divine.

What's Wrong?

It stirs,

The aching
Pounding in my head
Forever constant
Why?
What's wrong with me?
It stirs,
My vision faded and blurry,
Yet I can see
What's happening?
Doctors, never knowing what's the cause
Testing, always testing
I have nothing left in me

It stirs,

Weakness and nausea
No appetite do I have
My body, no longer in my control
Doubt
The fear
Not knowing what I'm facing
Asking the questions
They dance with excuses
No sense to me do they make

Worry
I worry
Too young am I to feel this way
Technology
We've come so far
Yet doctors still have no answer
"Let's try this"
"Try this pill"
No salvation can I find
The pain
The not knowing

It stirs.

Love

Destiny

In a dream you came
In a flash you were gone
Every dream the same
My feelings strong.

Where can I find you?
Where are you now?
I want to be with you
I'll find you somehow.

By chance we found each other
Unaware of whom we were
Realizing we love one another
Now, to stay together.

I love you so much
That's not a doubt
To share our touch
That's what love is about.

Never leave me
Our love is strong
Stay beside me
Here is where we belong.

Fearless Passion

When I hear your name
A fire sparks
A surge within begins
Your touch so gentle
Your lips I desire
Touch me
Oh, wrapped in this passion
I so long for your moment
Every stroke of your tongue
Your hair in my grasp
My nails digging into your skin
Love me
Gentle at first
Then begin your feast
I surrender to your will
Do as you wish
My body yearning for every touch
Moment of ecstasy
A rush flowing between us
Harder, tighter is our grasp upon us
Harsh kisses
My bite
Fearless.

Finally Found

Looking out across the horizon so blue
In happy colors with shades of pink, blue, and golden hues
Seeing the rolling hills for miles away
I can barely see where the tree lines stop
Trees rooted deeply, magnificent sentinels, of great height
On a journey I embark
With so many things running through my mind
As a deeper insight begins to unfold
Rambling in the inner recesses of my soul
The sweetest love I ever knew
Was the love I felt when I met you
You gave me all I ever wanted and so much more
That flirty twinkle in your eye and sincere smile embedded in my mind's view
Our passion and devotion was no longer lust
A treasured moment lost in love when I was alone with you
Know that without you now, I could never be
The sun, stars, and moon will forever be
The beauty that lovers can only see
I have finally found now what makes me whole
For you were the missing part of my soul.

For You

A baby is what they asked for
A blessed creature they were given
A sight that is so beautiful
A child who brought tears to their eyes.

You are this child
A gift in which God has sent
Your presence a blessing
A blessing we do not take mildly.

For you I write this
You who are dear to my heart
Wishing you the best in life
By your side, you will always find me.

Forever and Ever

They say *forever* is a serious time
Can your heart say *forever*?
Can your mind say *forever*?
Yet you're not alone
Can their heart say the same?
Can their mind say the same?
We use forever and ever so many a time
Yet I wonder my love
Will you forever and ever be mine?
I can make that promise
For my heart will not wander
My mind is settled and will never wonder
Forever and ever my words are true
Forever and ever my heart, mind, and love belong to you.

… Venisia Gonzalez

Found

Am I able to see?
The beauty that's left in me
The strength I once relied on
Love is far from me
My empty hollow shell
I need to fill once again
Can I?
I once invested all my love
Gave it to him willingly
So much did I glow
This enormous light from within
Oh, do I love him still
Longing for him still
Needing him
He keeps me at arm's length
A best friend, a lover but not a companion
Not what I seek
I need more than that
Great lover is he
No argument about that
Still, I need more
Must open myself to find me
Seeking who I am again
Beautiful, funny, intelligent, talented me
Loving, loyal, passionate me
I remember who she is
I am her, the woman that I knew
I stand before you once again.

Just Know

When times get hard
When you get scared
Always know I will be there
To hold your hands and let you cry
Know I'll always be there by your side.

♥ Love Is a Struggle ♥

How many times have you said
"I love you"
How many times have you heard
"I love you"
Does the phrase "I love you" mean anything
anymore

♥

How many times have you said
"forever"
How many times have you heard
"forever"
Does the word "forever" mean anything
anymore

♥

How many times have you broke
a heart
How many times has your
heart
been broken
Does your heart even feel
anymore

♥

Love is supposed to be joyful
Love is supposed to make you feel whole
Love can be painful
Love can be destructive

♥

How do you know if he's
the right one
How do you know if she's
the right one
Can you even tell the difference
anymore

♥

Love should be blissful
Love should be passionate
Love shouldn't be suffocating
Love shouldn't be a struggle
anymore

♥

Venisia Gonzalez

Needing

With all the things you seem to do
She still manages to be in love with you
The cruel things you seem to say
Her love for you remains the same
If your support was all she needed
You'd still take it away from her
A piece of you, a piece of her
That's what your miracle will be
By her side is what she wishes
With all that she wants,
      she made a list
A list for you to truly understand
What it means to be a man
Through this journey she needs you here
To hold your miracle so dear
Do not make her walk alone
Your miracle within her grows
As her love for you will never change.

New

Though we are miles apart
I imagine your smiling eyes so blue
I am swept with stars
So naïve is my love
To think for once you'd cherish my heart
For wishing heavenly blessings bestowed
To smile on an imaginary romantic love
Fire dying down but not destroyed
Dreaming of when the moon shines above its silver light
Wishing for but a portion of your love
Solace of pursed lips for the first thirsty kiss
The ocean's melody sings to me, with each breath of the sea
I focus my eyes to watch the sunset's splendor fade
The sun begins its slumber
To rise again in the morning light
Refreshing my love and spirit with new life.

Passion

I can remember how his hands felt upon my skin
Every touch made me shudder in delight
The way he would grab every inch of me
His lips so soft
Gently kissing every tender moment
Touching every muscle of his
The deep thrust of passion in every move
Perfect motion, in sync
Tenderness with a gentle hardcore
Feeling rising inside of me
Nails digging into the skin
Deeper and deeper in passionate embrace
Screaming, moaning of pleasure
Never wanting it to end
Lay your hands upon me once more my love.

Passion and Love Within

Tables for two with lights all dim
Ambiance permeating the atmosphere
Kissing you would be a sin
With you, my life would mean so much more
Being beside you my heart just soars
We travel to the beach where the waves await
Under the moonlight,
    we'll have a midnight swim
Bathing in love under the stars
Your beautiful face glowing
I pray our love won't disappear
Savoring these feelings,
    I hope they never end
The symphony of desire playing,
    our hearts it mends
We'll lie on the shore and take the moment in
A blanket of sand rests gently against our skin
Feeling your smooth body all silky and bare
As passion stirs deeply within
My hands frame your face,
    love mirrored in my gentle glare
I told you softly and run my fingers through your hair
Black is the color of my true love's hair
I cannot quench this fire within
I kiss urgently with no time to spare
Your fingers play me a love song
I linger in your touch
Deeply cherishing these wondrous years
Memories rooted deeply in my heart,
    never to part
My love is forever,
    to leave you . . . I would never dare
Watching love's color melt together through my tears
I love you always and forever.

Proof

If I traveled far and wide for you
Would you love me?
If I planted a tree for you
Would you love me?
If I sang to you
Would you love me?
If I wrote sonnets for you
Would you love me?

I'd travel for miles to reach you
Plant a tree so you knew that I'd love you always
I'd sing songs of love and admiration
Sonnets to be written of your beautiful face

If you held me
I'd love you
If you whispered love into my ear
I'd love you
If you stayed by my side
I'd love you
No matter what happens
I love you.

Remaining Strangers

You had this effect on me and you didn't even know
I could always hear my heart pound in my ears whenever you were near
There would never be a place so dark, that you wouldn't shine
I'd follow you almost anywhere
Oh, the joy your love would bring to me
Your laughter gives birth to joyful cries
I'd see you and want to swim in the deep sea of your eyes
Looking forward to all the times we'd share
All that would count is that you were there
Wondering, waiting, wanting
Compelled by your lips to have a taste
I'd move forward with no time to waste
I'd try to grip you tightly
You'd place your finger over my lips
What a tease you are
Dreaming of all the things I want to do to you
Passionately needing you in a physical way
Secrets we would keep of our love for just one day
Our hands bound as one
Bending over the couch in a lustful embrace
Our bodies basking in the sunlight's rays through the sheer curtains
Savagely we thrust ourselves in a passionate fire
Just for this time, I can say you are mine
Would these twenty-four hours have changed the choice we made?
Would we still never know one another's name?

See You

Your reflection drifts on the blue water
Echoed by the moon above
Surrounded by the vibrant hues of nature's embrace
So lovely
So lovely are you
Blossoming as love speaks through your stance
Late evening quietly awaits your every move
Lovely as all flowers
Crickets sing a lullaby
Your night-black hair flows like the heavens
Every step taken with a gentle flutter
You speak vibrant words as if on strings
Melody carries sadness
Longing for his return
This long moonlit night
You long for him most
Awake with growing passion blazing in your heart.

Their Fire

With outstretched arms
With open eyes
Desire soars throughout the night.

His masculine hands
Her graceful curves
Their gentle passion can often surge.

A gentle kiss
A warm embrace
Lovingly touching one another's beautiful face.

Holding close
Holding tighter
Very soon, they ignite their fire.

Venisia Gonzalez

Thoughts in My Head

I have thoughts in my head
Things have been said
Words that can't be blocked out
Feelings that can't be held down.

With these thoughts in my head
The aching of what's been said
The confusion can't be blocked out
Pain that can't be held down.

Having thoughts in my head
Wish for better of what could be said
Hoping that all doubt can be blocked out
Such joy that could be brought back.

With new thoughts in my head
Renewed words have been said
No longer need for any doubt
For love has been brought back to us.

Well, Should I?

Should I trust myself again?
Can I trust myself yet again?
I want to be able to trust myself again.

I want to be with you
That's all that I ask
To have me beside you
Is all that I ask
Let me in
Share your life
I know that time will show you why.

Should I love myself again?
Can I love myself again?
I want to be able to love myself again.

Every minute that goes by
Every thought that I have
Includes you
I know in my heart that you are the one
The one that you need too
You tell me so
With your words I hold true
Share my life
Share it with you.

What I Remember

I hide in my room and shut all the blinds
Holding onto days gone by
Hearing the falling of the rain
It deafens my ears, its roaring sound
My teardrops fall in unison
I'm feeling the tension, stress, and the strain
Encased in this love that I can't deny
The memories I've cherished, just everything
Thinking of you, my heart flames
It is a long lost memory that I chase
Not a memory I want to miss
That sweet memory I don't want to lose
As I take this trip down memory lane
Sweet memories dancing in flight like butterfly wings
This enormous feeling so divine
The wonder of you that made my dreams come true
Romantic thoughts begin to fly
It's only been you that I adored
With a faithful heart so loving and true
Giving all of my heart, there were no bounds
When you told me that in your arms I'd remain
I knew lying here next to you was where I belonged
Happiness and hope felt as if they were coming true
I felt that forever you would be mine
Moon beams that highlighted your beautiful face
I wanted to fulfill your every desire
I knew that I would do anything for you
Thought forever our endeavor of love together would remain
I listened to his music, my heart it did fill
Reaching and grasping his hands as above me they flew by
Expressing my feelings I could no longer hold
Longing for one more hour for my kisses to explore
In my mind I shall return again
These memories will reign forevermore.

What Must I Do?

What must I do, my love,
To show you that I care?
What must I do
That I will always be there?
What must I do
To show my love is true?
What must I do
To show I want to be with you?
What must I do
When times for you are rough?
What must I do
When smiles are not enough?
What must I do
When tears are falling down?
What must I do?
What must I do?
Baby, turn around
I'm here.

You, Me, Bliss

Loveliness beyond words
My sweet disorder is you
A lustful joy
Hidden with crimson lips
A gratified desire
Fire runs throughout my body
A sickness wanders to find you
Whisper to me the sweetest dreams
Tickle my bosom with your gentle touch
Arouse my body in a quivering dance
The aching desire to feel your warmth
A surge within explodes in ecstasy
Tighten your grip
Our bodies infused in a passionate embrace
Drips of sweat like pearls run gracefully along my spine
Shadowed hands glimmer in the night's light
A melodic ballet of movements and lustful groans
Joined below the belly
Lifting me once again with your hips
Finding you deeper in pink inner body
Rocking with the deepest breath
Grasping your gentle face as if a nursing child

Within this embrace, I feel your delicate, playful bite
Nails gripping your shoulders
To feel this exquisite pleasure
My face lifts toward the heavens
I cannot speak
Moving to what is the core of my need
Your eyes fixed upon me now more than ever
Gripping your thighs tightly
Arching my back
I let out a scream
Your voice follows with mine
Warm release comes from you, from me
Entwined peacefully
Soft kisses
Kisses from you
Kisses from me.

Your Waters

Let me drink
from your waters,
my love.
Let me taste
what your love
has blossomed.
Grant me the grace
of your touch.
Bless me with your warmth,
my love.
Embrace me within
your savage arms.
Tighter and tighter still,
hold me close.
Again, let me drink.
Drink from your waters
that blossom from within.
Your sweet waters.

Yours

You speak, I listen
Your words of delight
Sensual song played upon me
Hmmm, imagining every word arousing my senses
Longing for the gentle glide of your hand upon my skin
Pulling me into a savage embrace
Every movement of ecstasy
Your gentle kisses flow upon my neck and naked skin
Playful bites and gentle caress upon my bosom
United as one
With every movement
Craving your essence
My mind, my body caught in this rapturous affair
Do what you will
I am yours for the taking.

Uplifting

A Doggie's Heaven, a Doggie's Love
(Speaking through a dog's own words)

The most beautiful object I've ever seen
Such stuff as dreams are made
I am so happy to see you that I could weep
You in my life have made me whole
Naturally my body responds, again and again
I can't help the need to urinate, sorry about that
I know the truth hides behind your face
Though you don't have eyes
I can't see a mouth either
Actually, do you even have a face?
I've never seen it
Are you hiding it from me because you feel the same way?
But I don't care
You complete me
My faith in you, I keep strong
You're always here for me, and I'm where I need to be
I wish I could take you home with me
My master allows only our short time together
I cry inside, "Just a little bit longer please"
Of course, my master looks at me, confused
At why I want to stay with you
Internally, I wail and weep
My tears silent, but my eyes shriek in pain
I think my master is insane
Why can't she see my pain?
I'm ready to take the leap
With an oath, I'll swear to you
Tomorrow I'll be back if my master allows me to
I love you, red thing.

A Great Day

You're a very welcome guest
Spending time with you is the best
I'm making a fresh pot of tea
Offering sweets to the sweet
Cucumber sandwiches, pudding, and candy
Lovely confections always are dandy
Waffles with raspberry sauce
Apple fritters, blueberry tarts
I set the table perfectly
The patterns on my tea set you say look cozy
Comfy chairs
We sit, and I pour
Gossiping over tea
You tell a story that's so funny to hear
The roar of laughter rippling through the air
As we dine and sip tea
Time flies by
It's time to go
You merrily go your way
I wave good-bye
The best way to spend my day.

Venisia Gonzalez

Candles

Each candle I light
Is for every skipping heartbeat
For every breath I take
For every smile
For every laugh
For all my love for you
My candles light all of time and space.

Celebration

Come sit with me awhile
Under a bejeweled sky and moon's silvery light
We can breathe in all the wonders of the night
Throw all cares to the wind, come what may
Come along and reminisce with me
These years have flown by as you can see
Having wonderful conversations
Of what has happened throughout the past
We can sip tea and talk for awhile
Thinking of all that has come to be
Indulge me a little and you will see
As silken colors paint our treasured memories
Our friendships to last and never part
We will always be there with all of our hearts
We will be here have no doubt
With nothing to lose and everything to gain
Thankful for each and every day
I, myself, have no regrets
Memories I've cherished and will always keep
Unbelievable for me that's true
Made me fall more in love with writing again, thanks to you
We all are soul mates of friendship throughout eternity
We'll continue to keep this going as we play and write along
Thanks to everyone and even me
How excited we all must be
For we are now celebrating our anniversary!

Change of Plans

You've envisioned your future
Your plans and goals
Seeing different cultures
Adventures untold.

Then life had stepped in
Changing all that you hoped
Didn't know where to begin
Didn't know how to cope.

School and travel on the back burner
Children, marriage, and too many illnesses
Life coming at you as you turn every corner
Heels becoming booties, romance to tiny kisses.

Through all the unknowing
Your road, how it's changed
A new love that was growing
A new dream now was made.

Dr. Seuss, My Seuss

Would I
Could I
Just move on?

Would I
Could I
Stand so strong?

Can I
Will I
Stand on my own?

Maybe
Maybe
I will see.

See me
See me
Independent I will be.

You will
You will
Be proud of me.

Enchanted Awakening

(Based on the Myth of the Dryads)

Extend your hands
She will guide you gently
Enter this magical dream
Here, love knows no bounds
All of nature to embrace you
Let her peace and beauty find you
Stillness after the rain
The scent of life amidst the air
Gently with every step
The velvet-covered earth
May it guide you toward the tree
See in its soul her gentle face
Her branches lift you, her loving arms
Her gaze into your eyes
Opening the door to your soul
Let this enchanted dream fill you
As you awaken to the dawn.

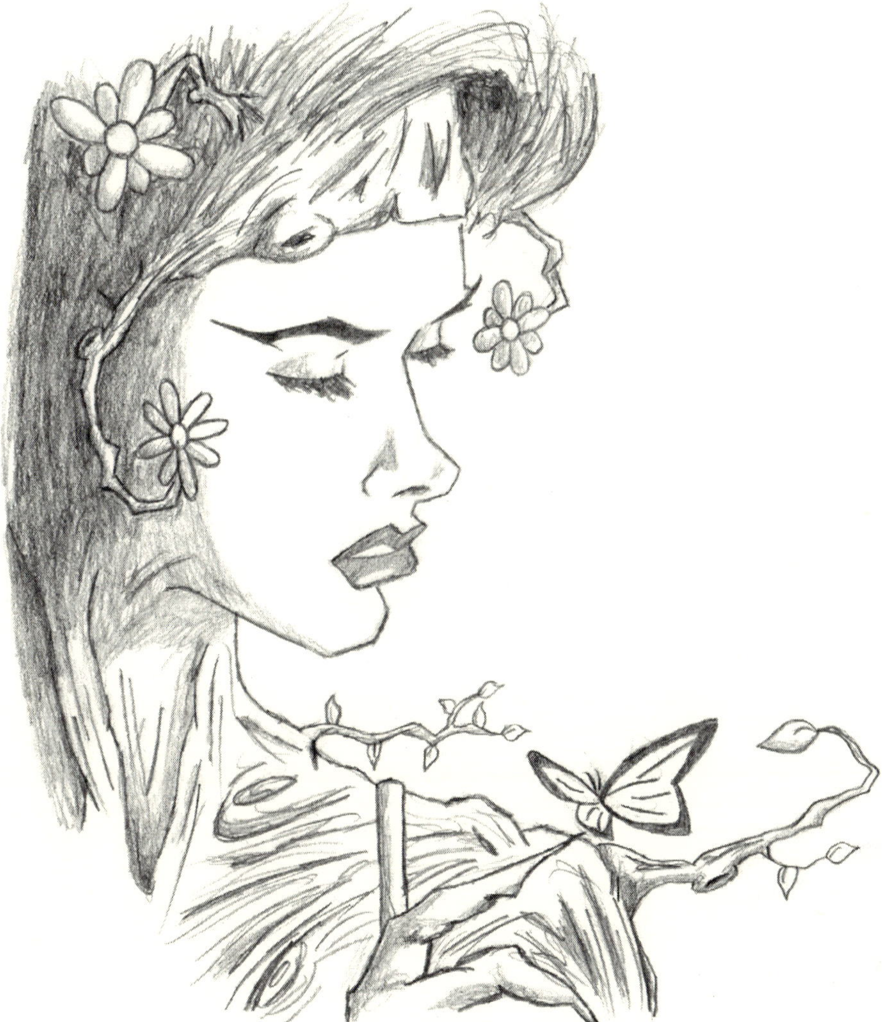

Heaven's Arms

I lie in the moss beside you
Admiring all the flowers
By Mother Nature's creations,
    I am in awe
Together we reached the stars
Now again lie among the brilliant morning glories in the early hours
Move me with the color of your words
It is my turn to hear the colors and hues
With glowing skin so fair
I look upon you
A golden light follows your every move
The winds of love blow swift,
A new sound is heard
Enraptured by the sound of melodic tones
Your voice too glorious for my ears
Now in your embrace
My glance will rise with you,
    as you soar to the heavens
Your delicate smile warms my soul
For love and warmth dwells within me.

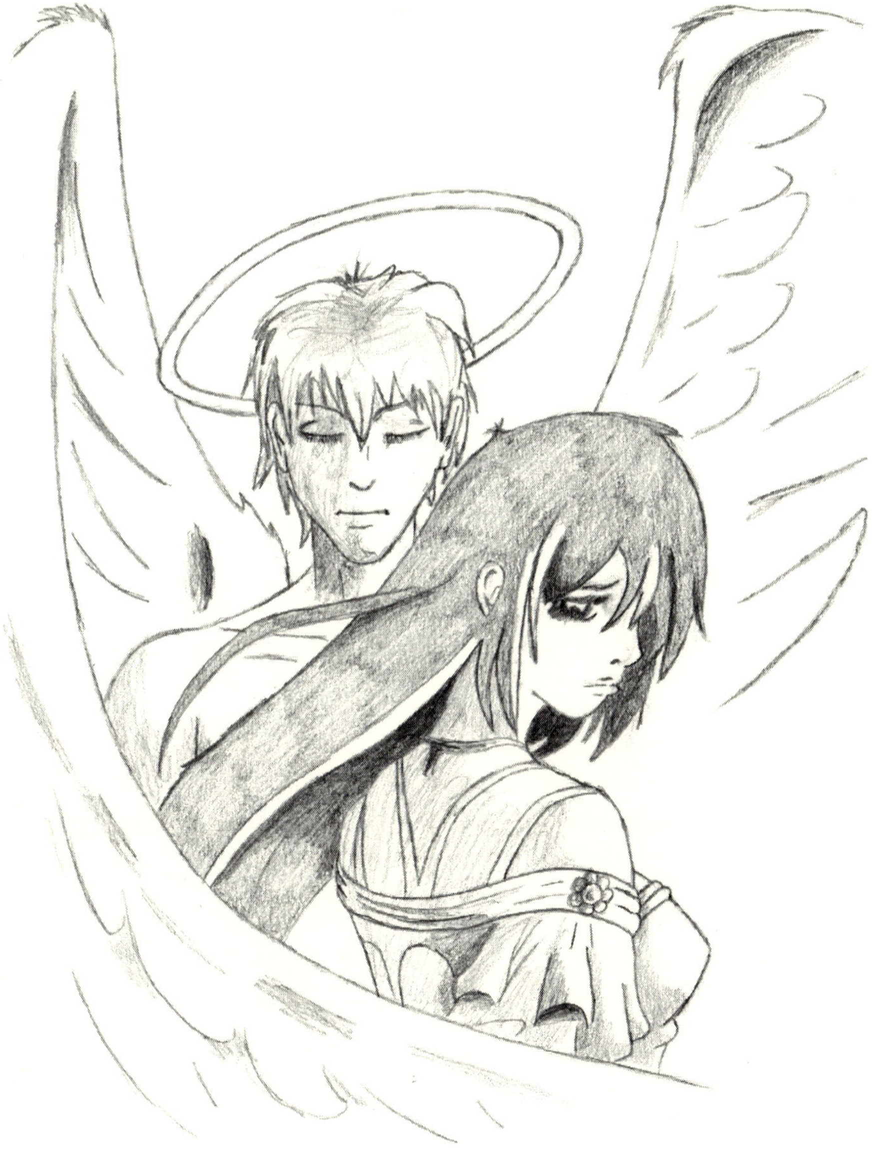

I Still Do

Show me peace
Give me love
Tell me the future
What does it hold?
Lend me your hand
Turn the light on
I believe you
Wrap me with words
My beverage is life
Purity of it all
I believe you
Look inside the garden
The garden in which I am within
Be here with me
Look beyond the mist
Look within me
You tell me
I believe you
I still do.

Is This . . .

On this cloud I wish to remain.
The thunder in my chest roaring inside my head.
Just the sound of your voice and I catch my breath.
Is this what heaven is like?

Linger

There I look above at the looming nimbus clouds
Blinded by the colors that peek through with a wink
It smiles as it lingers
How mesmerizing to see
I only wish to capture its beauty in a frame
To save forever.

My Pocket

Carried within my pocket
Holds desires to be seen
Some things are far too precious to be bought or sold
As some things are hard to go without.

Within my pocket
Loves are soul mates through eternity
Love being the greatest of all needs
That is what I believe.

Deep within my pocket
I fall asleep as the dawn fades
Crying eyes stream tears of fear
Through the sweat of vivid dreams
I awake from my own screams
Lingering in the doubting shade
Now weeping deeply and tormented still
Dreams that were once innocent can be no longer be retrieved.

Carried within my pocket
Music echoes through the air
Whimsical words whisper carried on the gentle breeze
I close my eyes and imagine when I see it, I will know
For my fears sink deeper, deeper down they go.

I reach inside my pocket
With open eyes, I admire the view
For now I know
I can change my heart and make it new.

Venisia Gonzalez

Nature's Beauty

What wondrous tranquility do I feel?
Awe inspiring
How perfect it seems
Clouds of color letting you know
Letting you know how you're not alone
Do you see heaven's grace?
Do you see?
What do you feel?
Heaven's face shines down
Wanting you to reach up
Lifting your hands to grasp its beauty
Take a deep breath
Close your eyes
Feel the blanket enfold you in comfort
Feel your body levitate with an open mind
Embark on a new journey
One that releases you from the barriers
The barriers that isolated your soul
Again see this beauty
Reach as if your soul were rising to heaven
Hold onto this peaceful grace
Blessing of nature's gift
See and feel nature's beauty.

Oh, Space, My Love

Shuttles soar above the Earth
Amazing to see
Beauty so pure, heavenly

In awe of the stars I see
Words cannot describe
Before my eyes, planets roam

Books no longer in my thoughts
My eyes see clearly
I wish to reach out to touch.

Peace

On the beach
Dark in the night
No one is around
Waves crashing on the sand
The breeze blowing
What sweet music!
Silk upon the skin
Close your eyes
Your body floating
Smell the crisp air
How I love the ocean
Freedom
Roaming across the Earth in great masses
Feel it
Serenity
Almost hypnotic
Your private sanctuary
Keep your eyes closed
Sleep
Remain in peace.

Petals

Lovely, lovely petals
Like velvet to the touch
Sweet fragrance you release in the air
Deep breaths I take with a smile
Oh lovely, lovely petals
Your beauty I do adore
Your colors brighten my every day
Each look at you, my smile returns.

Venisia Gonzalez

Rebirth

Here lies the caterpillar
Alone
Nourishing itself by instinct
Careful of its enemies
Moving along
Traveling short distance
So limited
Suddenly, a transformation begins
Slowly
Look at her encased in her shell
Safe . . . isolated
Is she trapped?
Does she long for the air?
Breaking
Evolved
Arising once again
Beautiful once again
Changed in freedom
Flight
Soaring above the world
Seeing in a new light
She is reborn.

School Days

So here again is that time of year
The time that I've waited for
Early mornings, then quiet days
I'll be able to let myself enjoy peace
Yet with this time, comes much expense
So much needed times three
Football practice, football games
Cello lessons bring ear piercing pain
Art supplies, artist shows
Again I'm a taxi
Car wear and tear shows
From 9 AM thru 3 PM
I find time for myself once again
Yet when 3 PM rolls around
My parental chaos becomes unfound.

For Moms and Dads everywhere

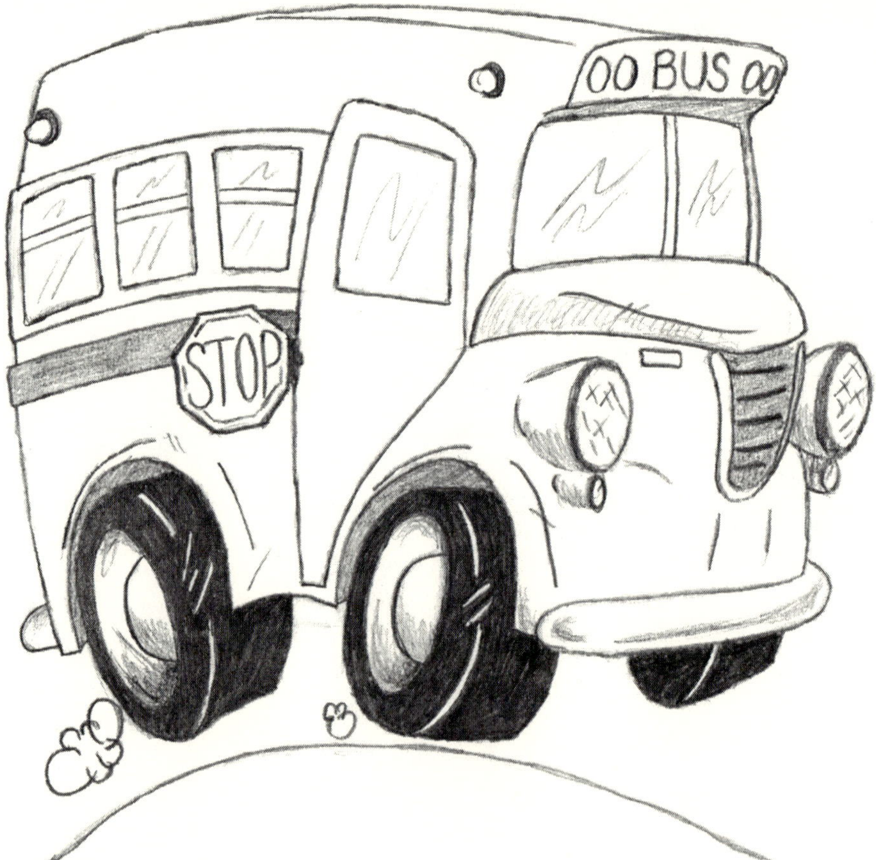
OO BUS OO
STOP

Sisters Are

Sisters are flowers
    that bloom when they're loved
Sisters are trees
    that stand when they're strong
Sisters are muses
    that give inspiration
Sisters are memorials
    with constant dedication
Sisters are teddy bears
    to hug when you're frightened
Sisters are tissues
    that soak up the tears
Sisters are faith
    when you're in doubt
Sisters are voices
    when you cannot speak
Sisters are everything and anything
    you need them to be
These words are for the sisters
    who mean the world to us.

Sullen Journey

Take a trip with me down my memory lane
Here I am with a story to tell
Complicated to explain
These memories still haunt me no matter how I've tried
To put them behind me, my pain to hide
Unrelenting tears I've cried
Hidden lies causing too much strain
Deep inside there's so much pain
Trying not to scream in vain
I've tried to soothe and heal my broken heart
The memories I've cherished, just everything
Now just mere reflections in my mind's eye
Your love for me made my world go round
Since heavenly love I thought I found
You lived in the moment, each day anew
Defying those who made fun and scoffed
Then finally with a thunderous shout
You didn't feel free to roam around
You felt confined as if in a box
I asked you gently, "Why, oh why?"
You couldn't even look into my eyes
There were no answers to my question why
You told me some questions have no answers,
     no matter how hard we try
With a broken heart, I cried myself to sleep
To awake to find you just up and left
You left no note or forwarding address
I cried, I screamed, and fell apart
I should've never given you my heart
Over time I learned to heal
Finding peace within myself
I now relax and let things go
For I know my tomorrows will be better days.

Take Some Time

Have you ever seen true beauty?
Just stood in place feeling the wind on your face
Smelling the sweet breeze
The bird's song, almost a melody
The sun warm, but not scorching
It's just right
Watching nature at work, peaceful with purpose
At home, the sound of a newborn
Gentle cries of requests and conversation
Tiny fingers, tiny toes
Tracing every detail in memory
How mesmerizing the scent of a baby fresh from a bath
Beauty found while sleeping soundly
    or admiring the look of amazement to everything new
A plant that begins to grow
The single sprout of life
Nourishment and care successful
What a vision
True beauty is visible everywhere
Just stop or slow down
    and absorb.

Venisia Gonzalez

The Night's Welcome

I walk along this path
Only lit by the torch I carry
The forest creatures of the night greet me
I walk to my altar
I long to praise the wind, earth, air, and water
Guardians of the north, south, east, and west
The black clock blends me into the night
I walk further into what looks like a black hole
Here I feel welcome . . .
      to worship the night.

Welcome Back

Lovely, lovely spring
How I've missed you so dearly
Ground no longer white
Your blessings come so clearly
You dismiss winter's fury.

Venisia Gonzalez

You Are My Drug

You whisper words of love
Words set fire within
Passion felt against my skin
You speak my every desire
Each word brings warmth to my lips
Warmth trickles down my throat
A surge within my body
I feel anew
My attention did you catch
I cannot move without you
I am forever yours
You are my drug
You are . . .
      my cup of coffee.

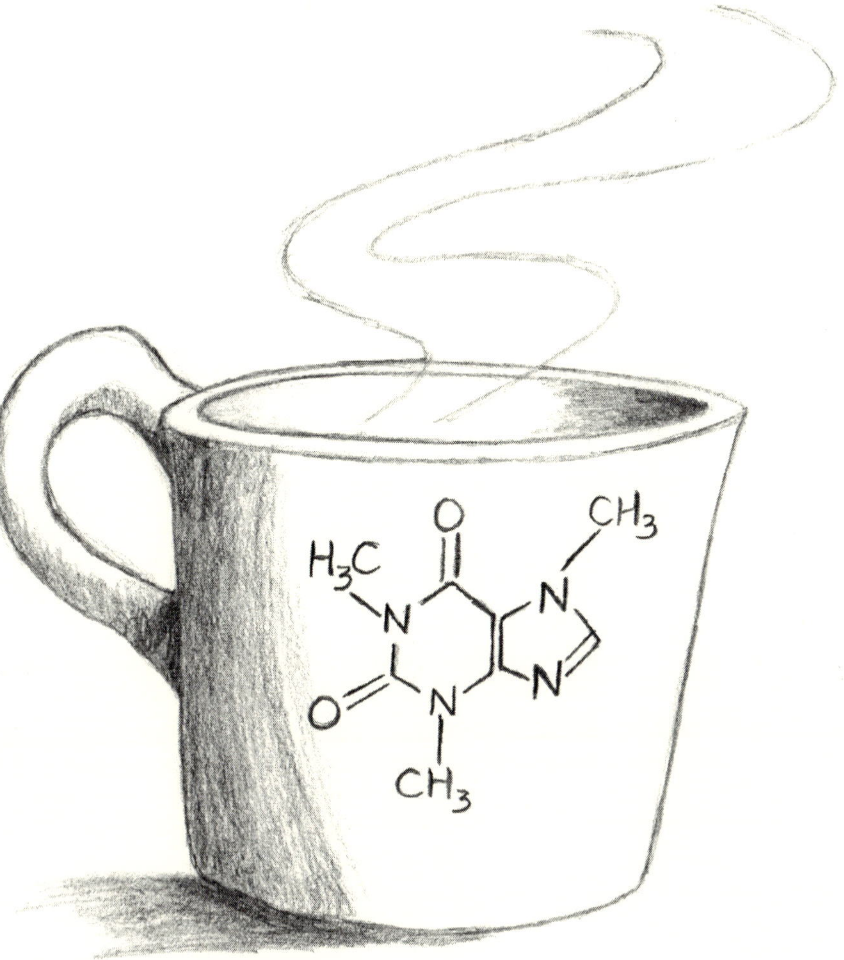
O
CH3
H3C
N
N
N
O
N
CH3

Dedications

Her Image

Those eyes so blue
I gaze upon
Mesmerized like a gentle song
Her eyes, those eyes
So big and bright
Could light the sky in the night
That face, that face
So round and sweet
Like a pumpkin that's good to eat
Those lips, that mouth, that gentle smile
That vision could travel with me forever and a few miles
Awake, asleep
So cute, so sweet
My heart it weeps
Her image, angelic and complete.

For my daughter, Isabel Simone
2004

I Miss You

How do you handle grief?
It's been almost two years but feels like yesterday
Crying every day
Missing her
Her laughter, her smile
The smell of lavender
How it felt when her hair brushed my nose when she snuck in my bed
My heart is broken
I long to see her playing
Hiding in a cabinet for hide-and-seek
Her kitten in her doll stroller
Her desire for being a princess ballerina
Dancing on the coffee table
Teasing her brother with the remote

My parents tell me I have to move on
I have to get over it
How do you?

I sit at her grave and cry
Wanting her in my arms
My only little girl
My mother couldn't even stay for her burial?
How do I mend my aching heart?
I cry and cry
Angry for she was taken from me by an illness out of nowhere
How can I make the pain stop?
Isabel, I miss you so much
Help me find strength till I see you again.

For my Isabel Simone
2007

If I Should Fall

When I'm with you, I feel like a queen
You treat me how a woman should be
You talk to me with sweet delight
Looking at me tenderly in the evening's light
The words spoken, sincere and true
Just the way you are, just being you
So I ask this honestly
An answer and act needed to do
Would you catch me if I should fall for you?

For Shawn Malone
2012

Venisia Gonzalez

Imagination

Little soldiers
Their imagination be
Scientists with experiments
So messy they can be
Lawyers, politicians
The arguments they can make
I sit back and watch
Laughter in my heart
Remembering my younger days
The adventures the mind can make
Bedroom—the castle
Backyard—their forest
Their kingdom have they made
Sheets become tents
Bathtub, their ship and roaring seas
Again I laugh and wonder
Wonderful the youth can be
How happy my boys have made me.

For my explorers, Kaelan, Dimitri, Anthony, and
For Dobie, their faithful, noble steed
2007

Isabel's Calling

Every time I close my eyes
I see your smile
Wishing you were here with me
Every time I look at the sky
I see your face
It fills me up with warmth inside.

As I'm walking through the house
I hear your voice
Your laughter fills my eyes with tears
As I go through your things and pack them away
It's your scent I smell and I'm filled with pain.

Help me through the pain
I know you're in a better place
I miss you every day
You were my only little girl
I can't believe that you are gone
You were so young and everything is wrong
I wish that you could help me heal
This sorrow that consumes me
I can't seem to let it go . . . now.

Someday when years have gone
My time will too soon come
You'll be there to take my hand
We'll be together once again
I can let go . . . now.

For Isabel Simone
2008

Venisia Gonzalez

Looking at the World through His Eyes

Looking at the world through his eyes
The shapes and colors of objects
Walking giants on two legs
Furry creatures on four
Wow!
What a world!
Are those my feet?
That lady that comes when I cry
She's okay
That warm thing
She calls a blanket,
    I like
She puts it by my face
That thing in my mouth
She calls a pacifier
I like it
Are those my hands?
Yum!
    My fingers taste good
Pick me up
What a life
I like it when she holds me close with my blanket
    cradling my face and pacifier in my mouth
I like her
I guess I will call her Mommy
I like when she rocks me and sings
Shh!
Mommy . . .
    I'm sleeping.

For my son Kaelan
1994

My Munchky

Within my belly
You twisted and kicked
Sucking your thumb
Relentless
Determined to come out
To explore the world
Upon your birth
A beauty and gift
Eager for life
So vast, so new
Full of love
A toddler you were
Sucking your thumb
Your arms forever
Around my knee
Mommy's love
Mommy's presence
All you wanted with greatest affection
As I watch you grow
Independent you've become
No matter how tall
No matter what age
My Munchky you will always remain.

For my son Anthony

Venisia Gonzalez

Six Candles

Each year that you're gone
My wound deepens
A new memory that will never occur
A new vision of you that I shall never see
Your voice that I shall never hear again.

Each year that you're gone
I pray for your guidance
I pray for your love
Begging never to forget the memories I have
Asking for you to always be with me.

Six years that you've been gone
The tears never stop falling
My heart never stops aching
Longing for you never stops growing
Yet knowing you're no longer in pain,
I find peace . . .

For my angel, Isabel Simone Fiorino
5/2/2003-12/17/2005
Sleep in heavenly peace, my love
2011

Tearful Silence

The beeps from the machines
The loud compressing sound from the respirator
It's cold in this room
No privacy
Doors of shatterproof glass divide us from everyone else
Tubes everywhere
High, low, in every part of you, even your head
How can so many tubes fit in your tiny body?
A cryptic toddler version of a Frankenstein film
You're no longer recognizable with what they've done
Stripped bare to your skin, only covered by blankets
They say it's easier to "treat" you
I can only hold your hands, your feet
I can brush my hands across your face
I cannot hold you in my arms
I ask you to open your eyes
I pray for you to open your eyes
I taste the salty tears that drip from my eyes
The doctors say you're gone
Kept alive only by machines
I wasn't able to make that dreaded decision
Yet, once it was made
It was the only time I had left to hold you
To hold you until your heart went silent.

For my Isabel Simone

The Team

Being on the bottom of the list
You're the bottom line to hold them back
You have to have passion
Unquenchable thirst
Tomorrow always has many paths
Which one do I choose?
The one that won't give us the blues
I cannot take a step into tomorrow
Right now, this moment I'm focused
Our paths will cross someday was what I thought
Yet now,
     this day,
          our paths have led us here
Wiping our sweat falling along our face,
     on our knees
Always wear that silly grin
Make sure your smile shows not your sorrow
My heart is home and I'll never stay
My love grows more for this moment day by day
Our eyes piercing deep,
     our focus illuminates
To you I make this solemn vow
I stand behind you all the way.

For my son Dimitri
2009

Without Saying

It's without saying how my heart beats
Our eyes that meet for the first time
May cause it to skip a beat.

It's without saying how love can blossom
A growing passion surges from within
May cause it to provide a lustful grin.

It's without saying how I long for you
My body wanting what only you can do
May cause me to explode with the touch of your hand.

It's without saying that staring into your oceanic eyes
I'm mesmerized into a heavenly bliss
May cause this ability of floating.

It's without saying that your words are hypnotic
I'll fall under your spell
May cause me to follow you anywhere.

It's without saying that you love me
Your actions prove time and time again
May cause me to love you always and forever.

For Shawn Malone
2012

Short Story

Abuse

A Short Story

Screaming was always around me. Tears running down my face, trying to silence his voice, her voice with my hands. Good touch, bad touch, I was too young really to know. All the poking hurt my body; I was in so much pain.

"Hurt me, not my brother," I'd beg. Hating bath time and terrified of bedtime. Liquor, the smell of his breath. I tried to imagine I was dreaming. It wasn't me but another little girl. That's what I'd try to think.

Trying to hide from teacher's looks, I always wanted my daddy to come and take me away. My mother left my brother and me here in this cold place. They were strangers, cruel people. Their oldest daughter never liked it when it was my bed she came to. She made me pay, but I didn't understand why. I was a baby. My mother didn't know. Did she know? Why were we left here?

When we lived with our mother in New Jersey, all she did was yell, scream, and curse. I was like my daddy. I wasn't a "normal child" in junior high, so she hated me. I didn't care, I hated her. It was because of her, her doing, that I was violated, beaten. She didn't care. "I should've had an abortion. You'll never make it in life," she'd always say to me. I wished my brother and I would've been with my daddy.

I wished we were with someone safe, who loved us the right way. We would have been safe. She'd yell at everyone, for any reason. She'd beat on you something fierce. She hated that I only wanted my daddy. I begged him to take us away. "Please, Daddy! We don't want to go back. Please, Daddy!" She had her ways.

Cleaning had to be done her way, and that was that. Laundry, garbage, ironing, hanging clothes on hangers. The ways things were folded and put away, the vacuuming, making dinner, dishes . . . If I didn't do it right "her way," I'd get hit with whatever was within her grasp. A whiffle ball bat, a hot iron on my right thigh, a phone thrown in my face. "Slut, slut, slut." That was her nickname for me (even though I was a virgin). I'd never get my high school diploma.

She kicked me out of the house right before senior year finals. My ex-boyfriend's mother welcomed me into her home. She took me in, no questions asked. Disgusted with what my "mother" had done to my face for the *very last time*, for this time, I fought back. His mother didn't want all my hard work over the past four years to count for nothing. My daddy was sending her money to help with my expenses since he lived out of state. Due to her and my ex-boyfriend, I had the opportunity to take my final tests, and she was even driving me every day to school.

On graduation day, I got ready with my new "mother." A gift from my daddy and her—a new outfit to look my best. Cap and gown, services ending with diplomas. Then here comes this woman saying, "I knew you could do it!"

To my curiosity, I turned and asked, "Why?"

"My baby is going to a good college because I pushed her to succeed. I'm so proud of you," she said proudly.

I almost vomited. I then told her it was because of my ex-boyfriend's mother, my guidance counselor, my daddy, and *me*. I succeeded because of me—for me!

I never wanted to be her: a failure, a tyrant, an unfaithful spouse, a person who'd feed on her young and others, an abuser. She was never worthy of the name "mother." She would never be *my* mother. I would, and could, never be her. I'm afraid that sometimes I can act like her. I want to be better than who she is. I feel in my heart that I'm a better mother to my children than she ever could be. I yell, even scream at times.

This was new behavior, and it started when my daughter died. I want to be strong. I want to control my moods. I want to be better for my children. I want to be better for me.

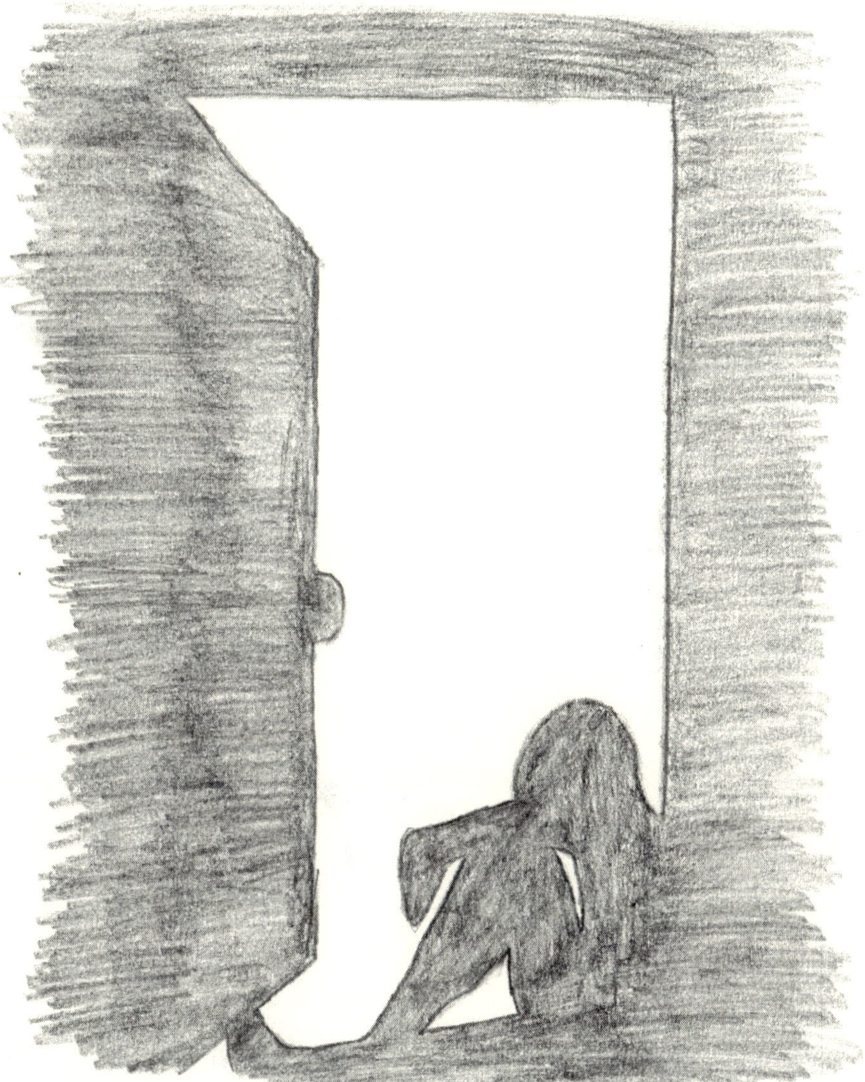

His Calm

A Short Story

The days grew longer as the weather got warmer. Sitting in his room, he wondered what to do. Looking outside with the sun calling his name, he knew it was a great day to venture into unknown territories of his mind and soul. The large weeping willow tree was the greatest spot to ponder his thoughts.

"I shall discover my soul and allow my heart to speak to my pen," he said to himself.

He put on his favorite pair of khaki cargo shorts and T-shirt then went to his desk to gather up his journal, which had seen better days. It was navy blue, leather bound, torn and tattered at the binding and edging. The paper edgings were all bent in one direction from being folded more than once or twice. He grabbed his pens—*at least three*, he thought to himself—and his favorite cap, and out the bedroom door he went.

No shoes were needed today. Though it was warm and sunny, the grass was cool to the touch. His bare feet felt comfortable as he walked across the field. There in the distance was the weeping willow tree, "his" tree, where he'd sit and write his thoughts. Yes, today was a good day for writing.

Once he sat on the cool ground, he closed his eyes and allowed his mind to open to the universe of words and began to write. His pen flowed like the gentle breeze, allowing his heart to sing words for his love. But who was she? What was she? Why did she have such an effect on him?

"Within my heart, my soul knows no other love but for her. She is the light in my darkness, the calm to my restless soul. She speaks to me in riddled tongue, which I cannot understand, but I sense her wisdom. Her power over me is exhilarating. The pride I feel when I am with her is like no other. She owns me, yet I own her. Her vibrations enwrap me in a trance. I love her like no other. I love you, my Camaro!" he wrote with such passion.

Having your first car—nonetheless a Camaro—is exciting! The thrill and the pride you feel is intense, and he was engulfed in such joy all he could do was write about his car. As silly as it sounds, writing about your first car is not typical. But he didn't care; he was overjoyed. Working long hours at the mall wasn't what he wanted to do, but he was determined to work hard to save up enough money to purchase his car on his own. The purpose of buying his vehicle on his own was of great importance.

Once he earned enough money, he went to the dealership to look at vehicles. There was so many to choose from. It was overwhelming, but he knew what he wanted: a Camaro. The salesman was quite helpful and understood what he wanted at the price he was willing to pay. After working out all the details, the payment made, the car was his. This was it—the moment he was waiting for, the reason he worked so hard for so long. Now it all paid off; he met his goal. He found what would make him calm . . . his Camaro.

She's Hurting
A Short Story

She made up her mind. She'd be on her own. She'd isolate herself from all of them. "I don't want to be hurt, so I'll let go. I'll be free. I want to be by myself. Alone in this world, cold and alone. Be on my own. Should I tell myself these words?" the girl asked herself.

"Don't stay alone when you're hurting, feeling so alone and deserted. All alone with no one to talk to. Be on your own with the pain. To have this helpless feeling, to feel afraid, to be left behind, to feel so cold—because love is so hard to find. To be by yourself in a small, dark room. Having no one to trust anymore? Having no one to love? Should you be by yourself? Be on your own, hurting?" she asked herself.

"No, I must find and love myself again," she said.

Truest Love

A Short Story

It was a decade ago that a prince had saved a princess, but she was no ordinary girl. She had been tortured, heartbroken, and betrayed—never knowing of love, not believing it existed. Until one day, upon an introduction, there shone a light of innocence, heart, love, and beauty. Here entered her prince. For the first time, she felt warmth; her heart fluttered. She had found her soul mate.

This was the time she met her love, her truest love. Exciting, new, like nothing she had ever felt or seen. She had been neglected for so long. Like every story, a love story, their love grew and they formed a union, ventured to new lands. Upon finding a place they could call their own, her torture returned.

Like a black seed that was planted in her mind, she was hearing over and over the voice that dominated her soul. This evil has torn this new soul to slowly turn against her love. Pain, chaos, and torment began once again—tearing their happiness apart, never truly knowing how it began. Fear was now controlling her every decision, her every move.

Despite her screaming heart, the evil seed was planted so deep, there was no path to retrieve. She destroyed her love; she tormented her love. She was no longer the person she once was. Years of damage left the prince with despair and resentment against his truest love. So believed, anger—such anger ruled their souls.

Their voices no longer recognizable, decision after decision made in vain, their paths no longer joined. Time passed, and he found another. The princess was never the same. For despite her armor and mask that was shown, she longed for her prince, for her heart to become whole again. Her punishments for her actions were illness, loneliness, and to never have love again.

Edwards Brothers Malloy
Thorofare, NJ USA
April 11, 2013